NECES

SARY

STRA

NGER

FLOOD EDITIONS

GRAHAM FOUST

CHICAGO 2007

ISBN 0-9787467-1-6 / DESIGN AND COMPOSITION BY QUEMADURA
COVER ILLUSTRATION: BRIAN CALVIN, *Half-Mast* (2001),
COURTESY OF THE ARTIST AND CORVI-MORA, LONDON / THIS BOOK
WAS MADE POSSIBLE IN PART THROUGH A GRANT FROM THE ILLINOIS
ARTS COUNCIL / PRINTED ON ACID-FREE, RECYCLED PAPER IN THE
UNITED STATES OF AMERICA / FIRST EDITION / THANKS TO THE EDITORS
OF THE FOLLOWING JOURNALS FOR PUBLISHING EARLIER VERSIONS OF
MANY OF THESE POEMS: *The Minus Times, Practice: New Writing + Art,
GutCult, Unpleasant Event Schedule, Typo, Colorado Review, 1913:
A Journal of Forms, Syllogism, Logopoeia, Konundrum Engine Literary
Review, Slope, Parthenon West Review, Mrs. Maybe,* AND *Conjunctions.*

FOR J. BRADY FOUST AND SARAH HERRELL

AND IF NOT FOR AMY

I would not be here learning what to say

CONTENTS

Things are not what they are—

EMILY DICKINSON

*In the background of every mirror
there squats a photographer.*

RAMÓN GÓMEZ DE LA SERNA

Things are not what they are—

EMILY DICKINSON

In the background of every mirror
there squats a photographer.

RAMÓN GÓMEZ DE LA SERNA

NECESSARY STRANGER

1984

Look at the sky, go
back inside. Cocaine
makes its way to Wisconsin.

The T V's thick with burial, hilarious
with seed, and while the moon,
my mind, and the real world stay home,

I will walk walk
walk unkilled around
a new year's clumsy gallows.

Anything's impossible. I'm not
you. Here's to music
to be in the movies to.

JUMP

A wind comes. We stand in it.
We stand in said wind
and under starlight,
much of which might
well not exist.

Word for dead
for word we are
the distance, flames
in snow. God,
the body is odd—

the most remote and unacceptable
of luxuries, in fact. I think
think think once
in a while.

for Joyelle McSweeney

PANAMA

Fruit thumps in the pointless
grass, has no hand in itself.
Complaint's a sort of orchard.
A summer flower plucked black's
another tool.

If only I couldn't
understand, I'd imagine
some sarcastic new Christ and say
something someone would say.

*

Pain is okay—
it's the practical
that murders.
Birdsongs now

in the trash-
thicketed blackout.
I want something to not
do with my hands.

HUFFY

August, the thick end
of summer where I'm
from. I've a grill, shrewd
tools, a bag of glue,
some Neil Young. (The world
eats what it orders.)
My neighbors cough and
wave and wave and frown.
Your youngest cousin
weaves by on a shit-
to-bed ten-speed, two
crutches tucked under
her too-white right arm.
This is to refer
to almost falling
from falling. It's a
dream I'm not ashamed.

OF WHAT SEEMS

LIKE MY FATHER

I met him in the candy store.
He turned around and smiled at me—
you get the picture.
Yes, we see.

You get the picture.
If it would all please stop for what seems like forever,
I could walk through spanking dark across
America on car tops.

I could walk through spanking dark among
these pharmacies, canyons, and flags.
It's not unusual to be loved by anyone.
The moon's got a fake side tonight, but still—

it's not unusual to be loved by anyone.
Wanting to hear what I don't want to hear
is hardly possible. *And then?* I'll come
to where what's said here disappears,

is hardly possible. *And then?* I'll come
and from an airplane jump
to open his piss-stained chute.
I am leaping like the pieces of a bomb, do you hear me?

Just to open his piss-stained chute?
I'm precisely the quiet of his blind spot's eye:
part heartache, part affect; part heartache, part arsenal.
Embroidered with cold—

part heartache, part affect; part heartache, part arsenal—
and to this sudden edge of city not a bird.
A border's bruised clarity, an ocean an ocean.
Try closing your eyes with your eyes closed.

BAREST GIST

The way the days gray
over is almost
a system

we believable slaves
blink back.

I move around
my many-cornered
heart some.

There are acres ever through me
flags refuse.

A NOTE ON ONTOLOGY

Mind could be a gash

is often riven
with whiskey. To wit

a morning filth, in that

in order to stop what I thought
was a rape, I once threw up

on an unsuspecting couple.

Hey rain
you old stranger,

every fiction is a wish,

the very best places to kill
yourself are beautiful,

and all the new miracles

are terrors, whereas terror
is clothes in a shipwreck's picture.

Some unbelievable slit of moon

confused through water
is an old face rising from the melt.

Our voices are all salt.

Our words keep ramming
into nothing into masks.

The sky is tar is grass is trees.

The ground is cloud is cold
is called goodbye.

JUST A VOICE

I could not be famous
to this place.

Pale with light,
I think here—

one eye small,
the other swollen—

and I look: you're always
walking. Your shadow

is a sky.
You are why

I say *entire*
life, *entire* world.

VACATION

maledicta Paradisus in qua tantum cacatur!

WILLIAM OF AUVERGNE

A brawl
of water, the sea
is not radiant.

One window,
light kissing at
its slits.

A brawl of water
is all
I ever wanted.

I will always never
see this again.

INTERSTATE EIGHTY

This world is conclusion. On a clear day, you can go
blind. The unknown is almost
interesting, with its infinite *I'm-not-
kidding*. Who are you.

Why is it we can't
touch when I so want to. That is,
to kiss and be kissed
slick, be gripped as ash.

Would you look at those trucks
of trucks—they're only facts. We've years
of brightest cold and fewer roads.
Don't yet be amazing. There's such a thing

as sentimental peril, you'll see. One needs only
a few songs, really. There's no beginning to decay.

RURAL MALL WITH

FLAG AT HALF-MAST

Helpful, a barn in the fall, a mall
parking lot. What I can see all

day: a system limping

through its grass, a spinning animal.
And that the question concerning

the problem is part of the problem,

and that now it's just the job against my hand.
I could change this into history and forget it,

but for the love of the love of a god, you do not

move. I like the way I'm still
not dead here, the way I buy

my way to environment. Soft

as blood begins
your corridor of things

and what to my wondering

eyes should appear,
should stand perishable there—

hard flowers, one hour, my film.

IOWA CITY

Compelled to pretend, I get
all elderly. As in *beer was a quarter*

and everyone would dance.

That boy is cutting buttons from
his jacket, sad miracle—that girl,

that one there, is collapsing a bird.

Graveyard. Graveyard.
Graveyard. Groceries.

I'm the only one on this bus.

MANAGED CARE

A person
may see uncertain
things when in pain.

Today's shadows
are rowdy. Their weight
is (say it): *bright*.

Flowers in a blue
glass, capable
as doors.

The sun erases
all the grass.
The yard is done for.

TO MY STUDENT LOANS

A stanza, a stanza.
A room, a room, a room.

Suddenly unemployed
I wonder:

how much per sway
is the wind worth today
in these trees?

I know and will know
that there is only
ever money.

Birds are money.
Trees are money.

There are only ever breaks
in its remaining.

TWO VERSIONS OF THE SAME

WATERY, DOMESTIC POEM

A lake unfroze and
broke—its water looked for us.

Dim spring storms clicked
our windows until June.

I had good news and bad news:
Love is trust in time.

You left and you left
an earring in
the bed.

I took it
for a little rearview mirror.

*

I want to tell you
I miss you—
you're not gone.

Your clothes are somehow
folded near
an overturned chair.

Glint, be it tin
or diamond
or idea.

It doesn't seem
to want to rain.

NUMBER ONE HIT SONG

The above is leaf-math,
a high
block of cottonwood.

I am for volume.
I am for tubes in and out of the sick.

If heaven were only
where only
you could hurt you,

I would touch its dead and broadcast
their entire range of breakage.

I would breathe to within
a skin's-width
of my sleep.

I would make a little nimbus there,
a clear heart for moths to toss against.

Late and unancient, inexact
as hands, I would move
as if by choice into my life.

CHAT ROOM

I've seen haste in vacancy—
so help me
so have you.

So help me the sky
above prison is a lie,
and I don't have a thought in your heart.

Oh yeah, the Real.
It gives me asthma.
Is dreams in which I freeze.

What's wrong is I can't
stop thinking me,
maybe.

What's more
I start to think you.

GOOGLE

All the fish look shitty
on their ice today,
the fruit like a dull
pile of metal.

A dead bag commutes
between the street
and the trees.

The sky goes
every way.

I never find you.

BALMORAL

Things'll get
all right,

the infield strangely green.

I can't tell you
who'll win,

who'll suffer,

how old
I wish I were.

It's always this—

just shoved into something
I never could have made.

AFTER ARETHA FRANKLIN

Baby, I know

but not much,
enough.

We are two
breathing people in
a room.

The rest, the rest

is as emphatic,
scratched out.

The meaning of a cruelty
is its hurry,
its use.

YOU DON'T EVEN LIVE ONCE

This is a song about quality
and that great gospel jest
we call knowledge. Say
she drops the bathroom water glass,
cleans blood from her hands
with a towel he slid under
their new designer plunger.
So she just lies there

now, feeling odd and idiotic
in their bathroom, her shadow.
She would leap, he's well aware,
at the sound of ripping paper.
He will walk into the house,
throw something down.

ONLY THE ASYMPTOTES

a sound somewhere

its airplane
somewhere else

*

songs aren't music

songs have to do
with music

*

all together now

all
apart

DEVOTIO MODERNA

Who but us
could know wisdom's cut,

the pain of pain's
leaving, same as you?

Who would smooth us to
a circle? You would. You would.

You and your planet. You
and your flagrant blue room.

HISTORYLESS

Near a crawling bruise
of river it
went something like,

"I couldn't see. And did."

*

Bad guitar, my next
capacity. I guess that's just
how a bird sings to vanish me.

How day and the bank disagree.

*

Leaking away,
I'll drop
you, shape.

Go ahead and feed me that hole.

BULIMIA

Deep one perfect morning crammed
with here's-

how-you-do-it,

you work dead.
Dread

is recognition

as is hunger,
throwing up.

When that glass cocoons water

you dream wells so deep
they've stars.

You've tongue without mouth,

a lace of late of crazy
so they say.

You compare, pale.

You mirror away.
When *I'm* sick you say,

"Say ahh."

I DREAM OF TEETH

Kneel on my face.
Today be huge
and strange.

I dream of teeth,
a whole night's worth.

Kneel on my face.
Today be huge
and strange.

Take the pebbles from an actor's
now-useless new shoe.

Get them gently to
my stutt-
erer's gut.

LOS ANGELES

Loss of faith is

growth is faith. The only critique
of paradise is paradise.

Be there drinking,

our shared throat shallow in all
direction, then nothing.

In this particular

version of everywhere, a movie equal to
and other than our memory

disappears. We imagine

wanting. And here, our wanting
is at its most tangible. The movie turns

into itself. What not for?

IN THE SPACE PROVIDED

On a near-
suicidally clear
day of wind—

a day like
a day like
television—

I wake to find
that a season
has been detonated.

Planet's automatic.
That tree's a gust
of blood.

SHIFT CHANGE,

THE OLD PINK,

BUFFALO, NEW YORK

I'll have
whatever shadows

you say
I've been having

for the last
blank elixir

of your unborn
afternoon.

Or human jam,
my body

of parts back, thanks.
That

and your nourishing
shove.

for Tracey Hamlett

WHY I AM NOT A PAINTER

The most difficult beautiful

thing I think
to paint would be

a close-up, a close-up

of a single square
of toilet tissue

floating

in a bowl.
Or so I'm told.

No matter. My bad.

There is no genuine thinking
without a sense

of indignity.

This heart of earth of mine
can only hear

is only yours.

PATRIOT ACT

Do let's be quiet and ancient
of a day, as is Earth with its endless
boxes and bags, its groups of good blue
and its river-worn stones.
A crowd amid monuments gets its.

How oddly rockstar we are:
animal. Animal.
And some unmerciful nail.

Them there hills. Them
there skeletoned beds. Them zeroes,
faces, ones, and thumbs.
Them Sony glass ghosts
stacked on pallets.

We're forever re-gifted—new eyes,
a shaky haze. (Them dragons at hand
as if needed.)

The sound of the gods who stay right where they are
is no masterpiece, no launch pad, no splash.
We just keep not starting over. The year wears away like a star.
I didn't. I didn't. I don't.
I do. I do.

As if turning (for Christ's sake!)
the key hard starts
the car.

BLOOD TEST

One's it
or in it—but what?

What's this:

your shout-out's
a shut-in,

the useless a fire,

some unbroken fuck
your new brain.

APNEA

Where was it
one first heard life

expectancy.

*

Mouth what

hovers above
my face, you hang me awake.

*

Just so much mythic bother

the first dream could not have been thought of
as such.

*

Paradise's insects
pinch—

and you can't notice.

COUNTRY AND WESTERN

The stars

here are hammering
the long-abandoned dancehall,

its floor adrift with ceiling, glass,

appliances, and leaves.
Take me apart

into my animal, darling.

I am not safe
to take apart.

I will sleep with you to breathe.

THE MENTION

you saw me
away

and when today

I've no one
else for shame—

I heard them say

your name
that's all

your name your name

it took
its letters

thorns

SUMMER CAMP

Haunted crotch-
shot, a slow
cloud scorched across,

ashen. Face was knocked
on into water
over rock.

I am in
a meadow, shitting
feathers.

BAR FIGHT

These two
are the clock of you,

beaten,
let be,

by one hand,
the other, the hand

after next,
and with the shifting

indifference of
a harbor.

HEREIN

A sober-dumb someone at home,
you'd like
to just injure these dishes, fist
a towel.

That backyard brain of mixed sticks
means nothing.
This pissy fence is nothing, un-path
to other grass.

You look up-and-gutted-
of-waves.
Afford morning. You are blind
as a mouth.

You are
inconsequentially shrill.

SUBURB

Thrown-up glyph
of moon, your smile
is savagely
exact.

What I take to be
the stuffing from
a toy
animal isn't.

AT THE MOVIES

I laughed behind
your hand

DAY JOB

What's it *not* like?
You're all memory, plight.

The poem is
the poem's is

a snag.

Your breath's a boned-
in thought—you don't wonder.

The unconscious is structured
like a bladder.

TO A BROKEN PAYPHONE

You, you
bored totem,

are out of your face.

I, too,
riot to

hear if I can hear.

GRAVEYARD SHIFT

For weather's crucial
trivia, we've crucifix
and waves.

Another funky carcass in
the grass spasms open.

Familiar hair there, despite the fact
that flesh at dawn
seems wax.

We're switches in the air
and here's your floor.

COMMERCIAL

Are you touched like a drum

or in a corner
cutting dust

Are you cranked across
the sky

Are you you there

MARITAL

To have and have and

have and how
could you not

stop blossoming.

*

Some days I can't feel
much of anything. Others

I come so

hard I think
I've bled.

*

You be careful if

you care for me.
You care for me

you carry me to you.

*

Our city's a list
of its pissed-

out-of windows.

Your eye (me
in it) is a dollhouse.

*

And here I don't

come, staring
down our warm

room's everyday blame.

*

Oh you know who
I'm kidding. I can't

make anything.

You break into belief.
I lie and you climb into tears.

FORMAL

Pretended you don't bleed. Pretended
to not bleed. Pretended
not to bleed. Ran cold water on it.

Meanwhile, winter
busied, winter
buried, winter

bruised. And doubt lit up
like some sudden and
unnecessary good.

APHORISTIC

Think back on that which
hasn't ever happened.

That which hasn't
even happened.

Now you're even.

PARENTAL

The two of us choose
or not for you to be.

Then music or not,
then weapons or not.

Then questions of the weather at your face.

*

Such little insertions
are often dumb as dust, but

we'd like to tell you how
incredulous that face is.

It isn't, but we know we could. It could be if we do.

*

Every sound's
its own ceremony:

a downed power line
for one. For another

this ice on this lake, fraying.

SOB POEM

Grief that we should be this.
I don't hate you, broken gift.

The revolution, too, is sad,
jealous with
and of its growth.

Whole buildings are devoted
to particular bones.

*

Start-to-crying's a wire from
the mind to nowhere.

Don't
just say there—signify something.
The leaves are on their shadows.

So give down your feather-
weight rage.

LIFE STORY

Plants push. The ground
bounces. The sun comes
up, a sweet nerve.

Scrapes of radio, small songs
of dying or of not,
just touch the beach.

I don't know what I like.

What I'm doing is stalling.
What I'm doing is staring
at good red meat

like it's a mirror.
Like it's something
I might already only believe.

AFTER MEAT

gashed arch of
the last of
your orange

POEM WITH HANDS

AND TOOLS

My nailed hand goes noticed, sure
to bleed to winter's floor.

This equipment, isn't
it for me. Isn't it all mine.

*

Also missing her's
a blister—a loud
pain, quietly made.

The loud
pain makes her
my necessary stranger.

Never mind.

I felt the need to mention it.

*

A good saw slips

calmly into wood.
Conversely:

me, a wind-up

device that slurs
its words.

CLOUDS

Such things
as laws fall on us—
soft programs, impossible models

unlocked into air. There
are nameless shapes.
There are tears of understanding.

"Here,
        catch."
Not a map in the world.

GRAHAM FOUST was born in Knoxville, Tennessee in 1970 and raised in Eau Claire, Wisconsin. Since leaving Wisconsin in 1992, he has lived in Santa Fe, Washington, Buffalo, Des Moines, Iowa City, and Oakland, where he currently lives with his wife Amy and his son Merle. The author of two previous collections of poems, *As in Every Deafness* (Flood Editions, 2003) and *Leave the Room to Itself* (Ahsahta Press, 2003), he teaches in the graduate and undergraduate writing programs at Saint Mary's College of California.